Make Your Own
Inuksuk

Mary Wallace

Owl

Owl Books are published by Greey de Pencier Books Inc.
51 Front Street East, Suite 200, Toronto, Ontario M5E 1B3

The Owl colophon is a trademark of Owl Children's Trust Inc.
Greey de Pencier Books Inc. is a licensed user of trademarks of Owl Children's Trust Inc.

Distributed in the United States by Firefly Books (U.S.) Inc.
230 Fifth Avenue, Suite 1607, New York, NY 10001

Acknowledgments

We acknowledge the financial support of the Canada Council for the Arts, the Ontario Arts Council, and the Government of Canada through the Book Publishing Industry Development Program (BPIDP) for our publishing activities.

The author and publisher would like to thank Peter Irniq, Commissioner of Nunavut, for his kind help and guidance in the writing of this book.

Dedication

Allan Angmarlik died in an airplane crash near Kimmirut, Nunavut, in July of 2000. Previously, while working for the Inuit Heritage Trust, he interviewed several Inuit elders to help us gather information about the inuksuk. As well, on our behalf Mr. Angmarlik asked the elders who were delegates at the 1998 Nunavut Social Development Council meeting what they thought about our book on building inuksuit. The Inuit elders responded by indicating that they had no opposition to our project, and that they supported it in principle. They did want to point out that the inuksuit built should be made for recreational purposes. The quotes of these Inuit elders were collected and translated by Allan Angmarlik. We respectfully dedicate this book to Allan.

Cataloguing in Publication Data
Wallace, Mary, 1950–
      Make your own Inuksuk
ISBN 1-894379-09-8 (bound)   ISBN 1-894379-10-1 (pbk.)

1. Inuksuit — Juvenile literature. 2. Inuit — Canada — Material culture — Juvenile literature.
3. Inuit — Canada — Social life and customs — Juvenile literature.* I. Title.

TT26.W34   2001   j745.5'089'9712071   C00-932405-4

Design and art direction: Word & Image Design Studio
Photography: Mary Wallace

Printed in Hong Kong

A   B   C   D   E   F

Contents

What is an Inuksuk?

An inuksuk, a powerful symbol of the Canadian Arctic, is a stone structure that resembles a human. Traditionally, inuksuit (plural) have been built by the Inuit to act in the place of messengers. Some inuksuit are ancient; they have been standing for thousands of years in the homeland of the Inuit.

The meaning of a specific inuksuk depends on the intent of the person who builds it. In the past, inuksuit were erected to act as signposts to those who journeyed across Canada's vast northern lands. An Inuit hunter might have built an inuksuk to tell about a good hunting or fishing place, or to mark a spot where surplus food was stored. Arctic travellers built inuksuit to help those who followed to navigate a safe trail across the tundra. Some inuksuit were built to

A magical scene: An inuksuk at dusk.

show the direction of the correct valley or pass to use. An inuksuk might also act as a message center, mark a good resting place, or identify an Inuit family's home.

The inuksuk has changed with time. Formerly, inuksuit were built by piling stones in a particular way, but not frequently in the shape of a human figure. Today, however, inuksuit are often built to look like stone people.

All the inuksuit in this book were built by the author near her home in southern Ontario in celebration of the enduring arctic tradition.

This little human-like inuksuk was built recently. It seems to be basking in the beauty of the evening sky.

> "Any person was allowed to make inuksuit.... I myself have made some inuksuit near Nattilik. Any rock can be used to make an inuksuk."

Adamie Nukiguak
(Inuit elder, born 1914, near Pangnirtung)

Inuksuk (Ee-nook-sook): A stone marker that acts in the place of a human being.

Inuksuuk (Ee-nook-SOOHK): Two stone markers.

Inuksuit (Ee-nook-sweet): Three or more stone markers (the plural form of inuksuk).

Inuksukkat (Ee-nook-sook-cut): Many little inuksuit.

Follow the steps in the borders on the lefthand pages throughout the book to build different shaped inuksuit.
Learn more about inuksuit in *The Inuksuk Book* (Owl Books, 1999).

Putting Together
Your Inuksuk

The borders in this book show how different inuksuit are built. Before you begin, think of why you are building your inuksuk. Remember that the meaning of the inuksuk depends on the intention of the builder. Is it a sign or symbol for something? Does it point the way or mark a special place? Perhaps it says something about you, your friends, or your family.

The stones you find will determine the type of inuksuk you build. You can build a single large inuksuk, or a group of smaller ones. Experiment by stacking your stones into different arrangements. Balance each stone as you place it. Remember that each stone can be used in many ways: try using different sides of the stone, turning it in various directions, or changing its order.

The human-shaped inuksuk shown here is made from nine stones: three chunky, rounded fieldstones for the legs and head and six flat fieldstones for the base, body, arms, and shoulders. Each stone is small enough to fit easily into your hand.

Step 1: This large, flat stone provides a smooth and firm foundation to build on.

Step 2: Two chunky leg stones are carefully positioned. The top and bottom of these stones are quite level and the stones are the same height. They are set as far apart as the length of the next stone, which will be used for the body.

Step 3: A flat stone is placed on top of the two leg stones. This stone is moved and shifted until it sits firmly in place. Since the stones have irregular surfaces, even moving them slightly can help them to find a better fit. If the stones are still a bit wobbly, a small stone wedge can be fitted into the space between stones.

Step 4: A second flat stone is placed on top. It is gently shifted around until it sits securely in place.

Step 5: Two smaller stones are the arms. The thicker, heavier side of each stone is placed toward the center, with the lighter side hanging over the edge.

Step 6: Another small piece of flat stone is placed on top of the arm stones to become the shoulder stone. The weight of this stone helps to keep the arm stones in place.

Step 7: A round stone is placed on top of the shoulder stone to act as the head. Usually it will sit best if the flattest side is on the bottom. If it feels a bit wobbly, try turning it to find the best side.

If each of the stones in turn has been placed so that it is balanced, then this inuksuk will be a sturdy one. However, if the inuksuk falls apart, it will be simple to rebuild. A repositioning of the stones may be all that is needed. If the stones are too small or uneven, or if the inuksuk is going to be in a place where it will be jostled, then an adhesive can be used (see the following page).

Adhesives

Inuksuit are traditionally made of precisely picked stones that are placed to fit perfectly with each other. An inuksuk built this way can stand for thousands of years in the harsh weather of the arctic tundra.

As you build your inuksuk, make sure that each stone is as stable as possible before you add the next one. Because stones come in all shapes

and sizes, some are easier to balance than others. Turn the stone from side to side and shift it around until it "fits" without wobbling. If necessary, you can add a stone wedge to achieve better balance. Still, an inuksuk that depends on balance to stay together might topple, especially if bumped. If that happens, you can try using an adhesive to keep it together.

Balance

Round stones are the most difficult to balance. Flat stones fit together more easily and form a more stable stone structure.

Sticky Stuff

Non-permanent sticky adhesives like grey putty caulk strips and sticky tack can act like a stone clay to help hold the stones together. They work particularly well on stones with irregular surfaces. To use this type

Building a small gravel inuksuk using putty caulk to help hold it together.

of adhesive, pinch off a small piece and place it on top of the base stone. Place the top stone just as you would if there were no adhesive; then press down so that the stones touch. The sticky adhesive will spread to fill in the places where the stones don't touch, forming additional support to help hold them in place.

A small flat stone inuksuk held together with white glue.

White Craft Glue

White glue that is suitable for crafts with wood, paper, fabric, and ceramics works well to hold together stones with flat surfaces. This type of glue dries clear, but usually requires 24 hours to set properly. Some of these kinds of glue are not very washable when dry, so be careful not to get any on other surfaces.

Building a Larger Inuksuk

If you decide to build a larger inuksuk, perhaps as a school or community garden project, be sure to have an adult to help. Larger stones are more difficult to lift and require special attention when balancing. If a large inuksuk topples, the tumbling stones could crush toes or delicate landscaping, so it is a good idea to use a strong adhesive to hold the rocks together. This type of adhesive needs to be applied by an adult using the manufacturer's recommendations for handling and ventilation. Two such adhesives are masonry caulk and concrete adhesive, both of which should stand up to the outdoor elements.

An example of a larger inuksuk that you can build in your school or community garden.

A Place
for Your Inuksuk

In the Arctic, an inuksuk is often built on a high place so it can be seen from a distance, visible as a silhouette against the snowy northern landscape or the vast arctic sky. Others are positioned so they can be seen only from a certain close vantage point. Some are located at a site hidden deep in a valley. An inuksuk can also stand along the sea, or in the middle of a vast landscape. It might stand alone, or it could be alongside others.

In your own place, look around to find a special spot for your inuksuk. This can be indoors or outside. Think of why you're building your inuksuk and choose a location that reflects its meaning. For example, if you'd like your inuksuk to serve as a sign of welcome, then you might perch it near the entrance to your home. An inuksuk that is a symbol of communication might be placed on top of your computer or near your telephone. An inuksuk representing balance could find a spot on your desk, where it would remind you to keep a calm and peaceful attitude. Or, leave a memorial inuksuk among your plants or on a shelf with family photographs.

Outdoors, you might build an inuksuk among the flowers in your garden to signify a place of peace and beauty. Perhaps you will place one along a pathway to indicate the direction to travel. An inuksuk built at a picnic spot could show that this is a place of plenty. Or an inuksuk perched on a deck could reveal a great place to see the setting sun.

Wherever you chose to place your inuksuk, remember that its meaning is the one that you, the builder, have given it.

Stones:
Instruments of Expression

A stone is a piece of the earth itself, formed by ancient and mysterious forces long before our time. In an arctic land of rock, water, and sky, stones are the material that the earth has offered as an instrument of expression. Stones can be stacked in order to communicate knowledge about the land and how to dwell upon it.

Round, broken, and flat stones.

This inuksuk made of carefully balanced round stones marks a good fishing spot.

This broken stone inuksuk points to the moon in the evening sky.

Inuksuit are built from stones that are accessible—round, flat, or broken. Each one is unique in its form as well as in construction. An inuksuk might be minuscule or massive, a single stone carefully positioned, several stones poised on top of each other, or a carefully balanced tower of many stones.

"Some inuksuit are not tall, while others are taller. The ones with the holes indicate which direction to follow. Some smaller inuksuit also indicate the best areas for travelling on foot.... The ones used for hunting purposes usually have two or three stones."

George Aggiaq Kappianaq
(Inuit elder, born 1917, Ukkusikslik)

These flat beach pebbles balance to make a playful group of sunny inuksuit.

Where to Get Stones

Almost all of the inuksuit shown in this book are smaller than half of your arm's length; some are only one or two finger widths tall. This size is simple and easy to manage. To build your own inuksuk, choose individual stones that are the size of your hand or smaller. Look for stones with flat tops and bottoms. They are best for stacking.

Red and black lava rock, gravel, crushed mica, beach pebbles, river stone, flagstone, fieldstone, brick, and lace rock.

Flagstone

River Stone

Grey Crushed Mica

Fieldstone

Gravel

Crushed Mica

Beach Pebbles

River Stone

Lace Rock

You can gather your own stones if you live in a rocky area. Be sure to get permission to pick rocks that are not on your own property. Look by the roadside, in stone piles and stone fences, and along beaches or riverbanks. You can even use broken pieces of brick or cement. You can also buy stones from garden centers, nurseries, craft stores, rock quarries, hardware stores, landscaping businesses, or lumber yards. The inuksuit on these pages show examples of some of the many types of stones you can use.

Brick

Red Lava Rock

Black Lava Rock

Preparing
Your Stones

From a tiny grain of sand or a little pebble to a large boulder or a magnificent mountain, stone is a part of the earth itself. Millions of years old, stone is the most basic building material there is. Most stones are fine just as you find them: pure and simple.

If your stones are covered in dirt, you can wash them outdoors with a garden hose or indoors with soap and water. You might need to use a scrub brush if you want them to be sparkling clean. Be careful not to wash dirt down the drain as it may cause clogging.

You can also polish your stones by using a rag to rub a bit of vegetable oil onto the surface, wiping off any excess. However, if you do this, you can not use white glue to hold these rocks together later because the water-based glue will not adhere to an oily surface.

A small stack of broken flagstone pieces.

Flagstone is the easiest material to use for building an inuksuk. It's flat on the top and bottom, and it can be broken easily into small, stackable pieces. Large flat pieces make good base stones. Long pieces can be balanced on top of smaller stacks of stone. A piece with a flat edge can be placed on its side. See the directions that follow to learn how to break pieces of flagstone safely to get the size you'd like.

Broken flagstone pieces.

How to Safely Break Flagstone

You'll need: flagstone, less than the thickness of your finger, clear plastic, a towel, and a hammer.

Step 1: Place the towel on a sturdy surface that won't be damaged by the hammering, such as a picnic table or a cement floor.

Step 2: Place the flagstone on top of the towel and cover it with the plastic.

Step 3: Gently tap the rock with the hammer. Tap again, a bit harder, until the flagstone breaks into two or more pieces. Continue tapping each of the pieces of stone until you have the number and size of stones you'd like. Always keep the plastic on top of any stone you're hammering to prevent small chips from flying up.

Materials for breaking flagstone.

Step 4: If there are sharp edges on the broken stone pieces, gently tap the edges to break them off.

Why Build an Inuksuk?

An inuksuk is a timeless symbol of our close connection with the earth. Since the beginning of humankind, we have expressed our thoughts, feelings, and ideas by using and arranging the physical materials of our environment.

When we use the pure, simple materials of nature to create an expression of ourselves, we can send a powerful message about our place in the world.

Five round river rocks indicate that this site is a restful place.

Three pieces of broken rock create an inuksuk that indicates the direction to travel along a garden path.

The sunset silhouettes these stacked stone inuksuit.

You can build your own inuksuk as a marker to communicate with another person. You might want to give a message of friendship or joy. Perhaps you would like your inuksuk to be a guide to a special place, a symbol of personal strength, or to stand as a sign of welcome to people visiting your home.

"During the summer of 1995, while vacationing in the Lake of the Woods in northern Ontario, I noticed some people had built a lot of inuksuit along Highway 17.... I thought some people who have travelled to the Inuit homelands had learned from Inuit how to build inuksuit. And so, I built a few inuksuit along Highway 17 to mark my own way. It's a bit strange to see inuksuit built along this southern highway, but...they are promoting Inuit culture and traditions and that's just fine with me."

Peter Irniq
(Commissioner of Nunavut)

The wildflower garden is a cozy place for this happy little inuksuk.

Balance:
Wind and Weather

An inuksuk is built by carefully balancing one stone on top of another. An inuksuk that lasts is made from different shapes and sizes of stone, selected and precisely positioned so the inuksuk can withstand fierce winds and weather.

The ancient people who built inuksuit also struck a harmony with their land. They lived in a time and place where a balance existed between people and nature. The Inuit hunted only for what they needed, for food, clothing, and shelter, and wasted nothing.

This inuksuk, made of small pieces of broken lace rock, seems to show a balance between the land and the sky.

An example of an inuksuk carefully designed to represent beauty and balance.

The inuksuk is the central motif in the flag of Nunavut, Canada's newest territory as of April 1, 1999. The blue, gold, and red colors in the flag symbolize the riches of the land and the connection to the rest of Canada. The North Star shown is ever present in the winter sky of Nunavut.

The Nunavut flag.

> " Some inuksuit are constructed with small pieces of arctic heather shrubs inserted between the rocks. These kinds of inuksuit are for hunting caribou.... The arctic heather is used to make the inuksuit seem like they are alive when the wind is blowing."

Abraham Ulaajuruluk
(Inuit elder, born 1936, Ittukkuvik)

21

Communication:
Messages in Stone

The primary purpose of the inuksuk is to communicate knowledge from one human to another. These stone structures are like messages left upon the land. They can communicate information to others across time and space.

Traditionally, an inuksuk might explain where an Inuit's ancestors once found plentiful fish, or, for example, it might show the way to a beautiful summer camp. Sometimes an inuksuk can actually be a focal point where messages are sent and received.

This inuksuk serves as a place to leave messages.

This silent messenger stands tall.
Perhaps it is telling us that this is
a safe place to be.

Direction:
Navigational Aids

I n traditional times, inuksuit were used as navigational aids to guide hunters across the vast tundra. Inuit had to travel great distances to secure sufficient food for survival. Inuksuit that pointed the way to good hunting and fishing grounds, as well as to safe travel routes, were invaluable. Series of inuksuit across the tundra helped to guide travellers on long journeys.

This inuksuk indicates a left turn along the pathway.

Looking through the westerly window of this inuksuk shows the direction of the sunset.

> "Inuksuit with holes in the bottom indicated a valley, or best route of travel, necessary to avoid steep hills, or impassable routes. Each hole in the inuksuk would point to the next inuksuk, indicating the direction to travel to."

George Aggiaq Kappianaq
(Inuit elder, born 1917, Ukkusikslik)

Respect:
A Symbol of Appreciation

An inuksuk can be built as a symbol of respect. It might stand as a memorial to a loved one, or to show appreciation for the magnificence of the land. Other inuksuit show regard for the power of a dangerous place where travelling might prove to be treacherous. Some inuksuit were built to honor places that had great spiritual significance to Inuit.

You can build an inuksuk to respect the memory of someone special.

This elegant little inuksuk seems to suggest that even the smallest things can be appreciated.

Strength:
The Sentinel
Endures

The inuksuk embodies the spirit of strength. According to Inuit tradition, inuksuit are sacred and should never be destroyed. For thousands of years, these structures of balanced stone have stood secure against the arctic winds that sweep across the sparse tundra. In summer light and winter darkness, these silent sentinels have endured.

This family of sturdy little inuksuit represent the strong connection that can exist within a family group.

This inuksuk was built as a symbol of personal strength.

"In the past, inuksuit were used for caribou hunting. Small inuksuit, at regular intervals, were used to mark a trail. These trails also marked the areas that were rich in caribou. There are also some inuksuit that are located around lakes, marking the best spot to chisel some holes for fishing purposes. These inuksuit would be pointing towards the lake. The smaller stone was closer to the lake; the distance between the inuksuit also corresponded to the distance between the shoreline and where a hole in the lake should be made."

Abraham Ulaajuruluk
(Inuit elder, born 1936, Ittukkuvik)

A Circle of Stone Friends

You can build a series of inuksuit that stand together in a circle of friendship. Like you and each of your friends, each of these inuksuit is unique. Yet when you stand together, like the inuksuit in this circle, your friendship creates a common bond of support, caring, and sharing.

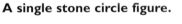

A single stone circle figure.

You'll need: a flat stone base, thin flagstone, small rounded gravel stones (for heads), hammer, clear plastic, towel, and white craft glue.

Materials for making a circle of stone friends.

30

Step 1: Break the thin flagstone into small pieces (see page 17).

Step 2: Make a small inuksuk (see steps along page border). Use a drop of white craft glue between each piece.

Step 3: Make several more inuksuit. Choose a number that represents the number in your family, or a specific number of your friends. Let the glue set for 24 hours.

Step 4: Arrange your stone friends in a circle on top of the flat rock. If you like, you can glue them in place.

"The modern, human-like inuksuit are made for recreational purposes."

Abraham Ulaajuruluk
(Inuit elder, born 1936, Ittukkuvik)

These inuksuit stand in a circle, representing the strong bond of friendship.

Index

Page references to captioned images are in *italics*.